Hanna-Barbera's
THE GREATEST ADVENTURE
STORIES FROM THE BIBLE

# DANIEL
## AND
## THE LION'S DEN

text by
## Christine L. Benagh

*Based on a script by Dennis Marks*

740

ABINGDON PRESS
*Nashville*

Two young friends, Derek and Margo, are taking part in a very important dig in the Middle East. It is the opportunity of a lifetime for them to accompany her father, an archaeologist, on this expedition.

Most days their young nomad friend Moki, who is very curious about these things, joins them to ask a hundred questions and to keep things generally lively.

One especially hot and tiring day, the three friends are digging in their assigned spot, when the sand suddenly begins to give way. "Quick sand," shouts Moki as the three

DANIEL AND THE LION'S DEN

ISBN 0-687-15746-3

MANUFACTURED BY THE PARTHENON PRESS AT NASHVILLE, TENNESSEE, UNITED STATES OF AMERICA

spiral down, down, down in a funnel of
sand.

Then just as unexpectedly the air is clear,
and they are in an enormous room. What a
spectacle! It is filled with treasure of every
sort—vases, jars, statues, jewelry and
ornaments, pillars, furniture of gold and
ivory.

"How magnificent," whispers Derek in
awe.

"Wow," murmurs Moki.

Margo has moved ahead of the others
toward a huge bronze door. The latch
fastening the two massive panels is a
golden scarab beetle. She puts her hand on
the scarab, translating its message: *All who
enter here go back in time.* Suddenly, the
great doors swing open into what appears
to be a cavern of light.

"Come on," she calls, and without
hesitation the others follow.

They step over the threshold and —

The three friends found themselves
standing in a lush, green land.
Everything looked pleasant and welcoming.
There was even a donkey cart waiting
beside the roadway. The little donkey
nodded as they approached, as if asking
them to climb on board. They wasted no
time. Moki took the reins, and Derek and
Margo jumped on behind.

They topped a gentle rise, and Margo
waved excitedly. "Look, a traveling circus
camped on the river bank!"

The soft air about them suddenly shook
with the blare of an elephant trumpeting.
Then a lion's roar, deep and terrible, filled
their ears.

"Uh-oh," gasped Derek. "I don't like the
looks of this. An elephant and a lion are
loose."

"And they're not tame," added Moki. "Freeze, everybody."

The lion snarled and lunged at the elephant's huge forelegs. The great beast reared in panic and tried to kick his attacker away.

From either side of the fierce combat two
men were approaching, each with a rope in
his hand. "Now!" shouted the bigger man.
And the two twirling ropes dropped neatly
over the lion's head. Furious, the animal
slashed out wildly. His roars and the
snapping of his jaws were fearsome.

It was too much for the donkey. He bolted and ran at top speed along the bumpy track.

"Whoa!" shouted Derek. "Whoa!"

"Hang on, everybody." Margo grabbed one of the cart rails.

Moki moaned and covered his eyes as they careened toward a boulder blocking the road. There was a crash, then a splash, and the three friends found themselves sitting in the middle of a shallow backwater. They were not hurt, but they were very wet.

"Is there anything I can do to help?" asked a voice behind them. A tall man, handsome and smiling, stood at the water's edge. He was one of the men who had roped the lion. "Perhaps you need a ride," he continued.

Moki just stared in awe. "You must be a magician."

"Now how did you know that?" asked the man. "That is exactly what I am." He made a sweeping bow and waved his arm with a flourish. "They call me Enoch the Enchanter." A puff of smoke and flame shot from his fingertips.

"Wow!" gasped Moki and sat down again in the water.

"Come," Enoch beckoned to them. "Join our band of wandering entertainers. We are on our way to the great city of Babylon."

"Babylon!" exclaimed Derek and Margo together.

The collection of animals, acrobats, and other performers was something to see. "This is Kalil, the animal tamer." Enoch pointed to the muscular man seated atop the elephant. The big beast was as tame as a pony now that the lion was back in his cage.

"We must hurry on our way," Enoch added as he helped the new members of his company mount a camel. "This very evening we are to entertain at the palace of King Belshazzar."

"The king of Babylon himself?" Margo was excited.

"There will be far more than the king himself," said Enoch. "He gives a great feast for a thousand of his friends and courtiers."

They rode for a while in silence. Enoch spoke again, "I am sure I will be able to find work for you, my friends. At this royal banquet there will be much carrying and serving to be done, but you will get a lot to eat."

"That's my kind of job." Moki licked his lips.

From his wooden cage the lion, Terribulis, gave another thunderous roar. A shudder passed through the whole procession.

Kalil came up to walk beside Enoch. "We must get rid of Terribulis," he said. "In all my years I have never seen one so fierce as this. He is a danger to us all."

Enoch nodded. "You are right, and perhaps Babylon is the place we could sell him. He belongs in the lion pit where they throw the criminals."

"Where they what?" croaked Moki.

Kalil laughed. "The criminals are tossed into a pit of lions."

"And then what?" Margo asked.

Kalil's enormous frame shook with laughter. "Then the lions are not hungry any longer, and neither are the criminals!"

Another roar from Terribulis underlined his words.

The sound was still in their ears as they approached the gates of the city.

"Babylon—" Margo could only murmur in disbelief.

The splendors of the great city unfolded living and real as they rode through the magnificent Ishtar Gate with its mighty stone lions. They went past the famous hanging gardens with tier after tier of brilliant blooms forming a mountain of greenery and flowers. "I can understand why these were one of the wonders of the world," said Margo.

Now they were going by the temple ziggurat. "Do you realize that this may have been the Tower of Babel?" asked Derek.

Then they were in the midst of a hustling, bustling bazaar. Moki was grinning from ear to ear. "I think I'm going to like it here. This is a wonderful place."

Margo shook her head. "I just remembered something that is not so wonderful. This city was fought over time and time again. It was destroyed at least twice."

"Oh no," Derek groaned.

"Look there." Enoch pointed to a group of people listening to a tall gray-haired man who seemed to be teaching them. "That is Daniel, the great prophet. He is one of the captives from my homeland, the land of Judah."

"Daniel," remarked Margo. "I remember. He became a very great man in Babylon, one of the chief governors over all the kingdom."

"Yes." Enoch nodded. "That was under King Belshazzar's father. King Nebuchadnezzar learned much good from Daniel and rewarded him with honor."

"But King Belshazzar has no time for learning or advice. His life is one big party after another." It was Kalil who spoke.

"One party after another," moaned Sakal, the chief caterer to the king. "I cannot bear it. There is not enough help for an ordinary banquet, and now I have orders to prepare for a thousand guests. What can I do?" The nervous little man fussed over the dishes, the glasses, the spoons and bowls set out on the the long table. He picked up first one and then another, looking for spots.

He turned his worried eyes to the line of servants waiting for inspection. "These three will not do at all," he barked as he came to Moki, Margo, and Derek.

"Of course they will, Sakal," said Enoch. "They are friends of mine. I will vouch for them. Besides, you are shorthanded."

"Oh, very well," sighed Sakal. "But remember this, if you make one slip in the presence of the king, I will have your hides."

"I'll have your hide right now," boomed a voice.

"Oh! You—Your—Your Majesty—my Lord—" Sakal kept babbling and bowing.

King Belshazzar picked up one of the goblets from the table. He looked at it scornfully and sent it crashing against the wall. "Do you think that miserable cup is fit for me or for my guests? I am the king! I want cups of gold and silver to match my greatness!"

Sakal was wringing his hands. "Be merciful, Sire. Where can I get so many precious cups by tonight?"

"That is your problem," snapped the king.

The chief counselor was standing at the king's side. He whispered into the king's ear. "Remember the many cups of gold and silver that you captured from the temple at Jerusalem, Your Majesty. They are even now lying in your treasure room."

"So they are, Nebiza," the king smiled. "You, Sakal, fetch the temple vessels, the golden ones from Jerusalem." He and his counselor swept out of the room.

Sakal looked more troubled than ever. "This is not good. Those are holy vessels, set aside for use in the temple of the Jews. It is not right to use them for a feast. The God of the Jews will be angry." He took the torch from a nearby stand and motioned to Derek and Moki. Margo followed along.

He opened the door of the great vault,

and they saw a vast treasure hoard in the flickering light. Here were the spoils from a hundred battles: rows of spears and swords and shields; chests of jewels; cloth of scarlet and purple; vases, urns, figures of birds and fantastic beasts. Sakal kept shaking his head and muttering, "I do not like this. I do not like this at all."

There was a sudden flood of light as the torch beam fell on a mound of golden cups and set them glittering. Poor Sakal was actually trembling, and his companions began to sense something of the meaning of his fear.

"This will be a great insult to their God. But I have no choice. You can see I have no choice." He carefully lifted one of the cups, rubbed it against his tunic, and held it high.

The goblet in the king's hand gave off the same shimmering light, but Belshazzar took no notice as he put it to his lips and drank deeply. He filled it again and again, spilling and sloshing his wine. There were gold and silver cups for all the guests, and the wine poured into them would have filled a river. Belshazzar's feast was lavish beyond all imagining.

The circus entertainers won applause from the reveling guests with their presentations. Enoch was a special favorite as he passed the bouquets he produced from nowhere to the eager hands of the ladies.

Margo and Derek had never done so much rushing about. "Moki sure does disappear a lot," whispered Margo as she passed Derek carrying a large pudding bowl.

Derek motioned with his head to where Moki sat hunched behind a serving table busily stuffing himself with choice tidbits from the banquet trays.

Only the king's counselors seemed solemn. "Our king does nothing but revel. We might as well not have a king," Nebiza spoke bitterly. "Our city has become a playground for fools, Alreth."

"What you say is true," the man replied. "At this moment our city could be taken by an army of jackasses."

The king rose unsteadily from his throne. "I propose a toast," he shouted above the laughter. "Raise your glasses to the god of gold."

A nobleman close by raised his glass. "O King, I propose a toast to the god of silver."

One after another the merrymakers drank toasts to the gods of brass and iron, the gods of wood and of stone. The music and the toasting grew more and more frenzied. Suddenly a scream rang out, and there was silence.

All eyes turned to where the woman pointed. A disembodied hand was writing with outstretched finger on the wall behind King Belshazzar. The guests watched in terror. When the hand disappeared, the words MENE, MENE, TEKEL, UPHARSIN were burned into the wall.

The king collapsed on his throne. A stunned silence hung over the hall. When Belshazzar could speak, he cried, "Wisemen, magicians, come forward and tell me the meaning of this."

An astrologer stepped forward. "My Lord, we are as puzzled as everyone else. We do not know."

"Come now," the king pleaded. "Put your minds to it. The one who interprets this writing will receive a scarlet robe and a golden chain and will become the third ruler in the kingdom."

"Why don't you tell him, Enoch?" Moki nudged his friend. "You're a magician."

"No, Moki." Enoch's voice was grave. "I am only an entertainer. That writing is the work of God, and only someone chosen by God can read it. Someone like Daniel the prophet."

"My son, listen to me." The queen mother came swiftly into the room. "This is a serious matter. You must call Daniel to interpret the meaning of it."

"And who is this Daniel you speak of, Mother?" The king's voice shook.

"He is a Jewish captive, my son. His wisdom and prophecies were greatly honored when your father was king."

"Bring Daniel to me," Belshazzar commanded.

The guest company sat in respectful silence as the stately figure entered the room. Without saying a word, Daniel strode to the wall and stood looking at the strange words.

At last he spoke. "These words were written by the hand of God. You have blasphemed, King Belshazzar.

"With the sacred vessels from the temple of the Lord of heaven you have toasted lifeless gods of gold and silver, of wood and stone. You have glorified yourself instead of the God of all who gave you breath.

"This is the meaning of the writing: The first words mean that God has brought your kingdom to an end.

"The second word means that you have been weighed in the balance and found wanting.

"The third word means that your kingdom will be given to the Medes and Persians."

King Belshazzar sat silent for a long moment. Then he burst into laughter. "A clever explanation, Daniel, but I don't believe a word of it. However, I will keep my word. Bring Daniel the robe and golden chain. You are now the third ruler of this kingdom that is coming to an early end."

The king laughed, raising his golden cup. The whole company broke into laughter, their revelry soon reaching a fevered pitch.

"Look!" Margo pointed to the messenger who came staggering into the room.

"Persians—" he gasped, "coming—only an hour—from—gates. Darius is coming—coming—with an army."

Even as he spoke the sound of trumpets could be heard in the distance. The banquet hall turned to pandemonium, the guests went running in all directions.

"I will not flee." Belshazzar rose. "Darius will find me in my chambers."

Nebiza and Alreth were whispering together, and the two left the room close behind the king.

"I don't care for those guys," said Moki. "They are up to no good."

A muffled cry came from the king's chamber. Daniel had been standing with his eyes closed. "The king is dead," he said, "killed by traitors."

A short time later the queen mother came in and brought the news.

Nebiza and Alreth entered the room. Alreth turned to Daniel. "If what you say is true, I suggest you join us in welcoming Darius. He may let us live. Come along, the sound of the trumpets is getting closer."

Nebiza started to run. "We should meet him at the city gate."

Darius rode peacefully into the city to the blare of silver trumpets under a thousand shining stars.

The three ministers stood waiting to greet him. The conqueror already knew their names. "Ah, Nebiza and Alreth, and you too, Daniel, I am honored. You are the wisest counselors in Babylon. Will you do me still more honor and continue to serve?"

"Without question, Sire." Nebiza bowed low.

"Darius, my king." Alreth bowed even lower.

"And what of you, Daniel?" asked Darius. "Will you serve as a governor and help me return this city to greatness?"

"With God's help, I will," Daniel replied.

The three young adventurers had been watching the procession from the shelter of an arched doorway. Presently, they heard voices—familiar voices—behind them. Nebiza and Alreth had retreated to a dark passageway for a hurried conference.

"If we want things to keep running our way, Alreth, we will have to deal with Daniel. He will spoil everything."

"I agree, Nebiza. Darius thinks too highly of him. We must get rid of him."

"I told you those two are slimy characters," Moki whispered. Suddenly he filled the silence with a loud sneeze.

"Someone has been listening," squeaked Nebiza.

Alreth summoned the soldiers standing patrol on the street. "After those enemies running down the street. Do not let them get away!"

The chase was on. The three friends dodged up one winding alley and down another. When they heard the soldiers gaining, they ran up a flight of stairs and took to the rooftops of the now-sleeping city. "Follow me," Derek called. "I've seen this in the movies dozens of times." He jumped down onto an outstretched awning and slid silently to the street. Moki followed and then Margo.

"Oh," she cried, "I've turned my ankle."

Derek helped her to her feet. "We can't stay here. Lean on us, and we'll hide out in some recess until the soldiers pass."

A door opened quietly beside them. "Come in." It was Daniel.

"Boy, are we glad to see you!" Moki dropped exhausted to the floor.

Not far away, Daniel's narrow street opened into a broad courtyard. Here was the fearsome lion pit. Early next morning Kalil and Enoch came to the dreaded place dragging the heavy wooden cage in which Terribulis was raging. They hoped to sell their troublesome animal to the keeper of the lions. The man wanted Terribulis the moment he saw him, but he did not want to pay a fair price. It took a good bit of haggling to reach a bargain.

Finally, the keeper gave Enoch a handful of gold coins and Kalil cautioned him, "Be careful with this fellow. He is the fiercest lion I have ever dealt with, a real man-killer."

"Good," the keeper gave a hearty laugh. "That is just what we need here."

Daniel gave his guests a tasty breakfast and excused himself to say his prayers. When he returned, Margo insisted that her ankle was feeling as good as new. "Do you think it's safe for us to go out?"

"Of course," said Daniel. "The soldiers have no idea whom they were chasing in the dark."

"Please remember what we told you about those two so-called friends of yours," urged Derek.

"They mean to get rid of you, no kidding," put in Moki.

"Thank you, my friends," Daniel smiled. "The Lord God will protect me, and may he go with you now. I must be off to the palace. Good-bye."

Moki watched from the window as Daniel left. A sly figure emerged from behind the building and followed him. "Hey guys, come on. Some creepy guy is following Daniel." He led the way.

At the west entrance of the Hanging Gardens, Nebiza and Alreth talked with their spy. "He does nothing wrong, my masters. He is honest and upright. He is also a devout man, and he prays to his God three times a day."

"Then—" Nebiza rubbed his beard, "we will have to do something about his praying. We will make a law against it."

The plotters wasted no time in presenting their plan to King Darius. "It will be a great honor for you, Sire." Nebiza dropped to his knees and touched his head to the ground. "For thirty days no one in this dominion will ask anything from anyone but you. They may not ask another prince or another god."

Alreth groveled beside him. "Anyone who breaks this special law, O King, will be doing serious disrespect to your majesty. He will be thrown to the lions."

"That sounds like a good idea," Darius nodded. "Everything must be asked from me. I like that. You prepare the law and I will sign it."

Moki and company had been doing some spying of their own, and they hurried to let Daniel know of this new danger.

"They are just waiting to catch you praying," explained Derek. "Then they will arrest you, and then—"

"Hide when you are praying," warned Moki.

"Do not worry, my friends," said Daniel. "In this foreign city, I always open my window and turn my face toward Jerusalem to pray. God will protect me."

When Daniel returned to his home at sunset, he opened his window and knelt to pray.

Before long, the door burst open, and the soldiers were on him in an instant.

Darius was stunned when he saw the prisoner. "Oh no, not you, Daniel." He glared at Nebiza and Alreth who were smiling at each other.

Nebiza came forward. "Remember, King Darius, the law of the Persians must be obeyed. It cannot be broken, not even by the king."

"Do not fear for me," said Daniel, "my God will protect me. Do whatever your law demands."

The unhappy king bowed his head. Nebiza waved to the soldiers. They took Daniel straight to the edge of the pit and gave him a shove. There was a heavy thud, then sharp snarls and growls.

The keeper called two men to slide the huge stone over the top of the pit. "It should all be over in a minute," one guard said to the other. "These lions have not been fed for a week."

Daniel lay dazed at the bottom of the pit. When he opened his eyes he saw the line of beasts staring at him.

Terribulis was in the lead with nostrils flared and fangs dripping. "O Lord," prayed Daniel, "if thy servant is found worthy, save me from these beasts."

While Daniel prayed Terribulis circled slowly, lowering his head, and moving ever closer. Another lion was now circling around behind preparing to attack. Terribulis gave a roar and sprang—placing himself between the man and the other beast. That lion turned and slunk away.

Daniel stretched out his hand toward Terribulis, and the great lion came near. Daniel stroked the golden mane. "Praise be to God, I have been saved by an angel of the Lord."

N o one got any sleep that night. At the break of day the three friends gathered not far from the mouth of the pit. King Darius was already there, and soon Enoch joined the group.

The king addressed the keeper. "Have your men remove the stone."

When they peered in, they saw Daniel lying motionless at the bottom. Derek, Margo, and Moki were stunned at the sight of his still body.

Suddenly Daniel stretched and sat up. Moki jumped with joy. "He was asleep with the lions," squealed Moki. "Wow!"

The king called down, "Your God has saved you from the jaws of the lions. All praise to the God of Daniel."

Then Darius gave another command: "Arrest those men." He pointed to Nebiza and Alreth. "Let them suffer the fate they had planned for Daniel."

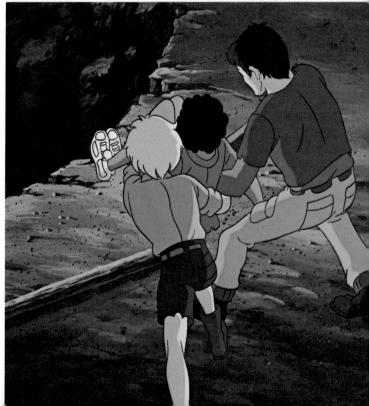

erek took Margo's arm. "Don't you
think it's time for us to be going?"
They looked around for Moki. He came
running toward them from the other side of
the courtyard. Just as he got near the pit,
he stepped on one of the logs and went
rolling toward the edge. Derek and Margo
rushed to grab his arms and pull him to
safety. It was not a moment too soon, for
one of the lions was leaping up to grab at
his legs dangling over the side.

"Whew," gasped Moki, "that lion was
trying to put the bite on me."

Enoch came up to say good-bye to his
friends. "I too must be on my way. I have
stayed too long in Babylon, but I am very
glad that I did not miss this day. Praise be
to God."

K ing Darius wrote a decree and had it read throughout his kingdom.

"Let all people everywhere fear and reverence the God of Daniel, for he is the living God who works wonders. His kingdom shall last forever. Let his name be praised."

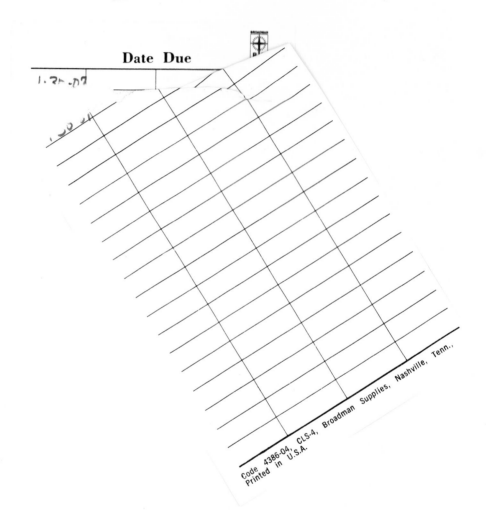

**Date Due**

1.24.07

Code 4386-04, CLS-4, Broadman Supplies, Nashville, Tenn.,
Printed in U.S.A.